POSTCARD HISTORY SERIES

Walker County

Huntsville is the seat of Walker County, Texas, and is known as the home of Sam Houston. (Courtesy of the Walker County Historical Commission.)

On the Cover: J.R. King and Company of Huntsville, Texas, published this postcard to showcase the city's courthouse and downtown square around 1899. (Courtesy of the Walker County Historical Commission.)

POSTCARD HISTORY SERIES

Walker County

Jeffrey L. Littlejohn and the
Walker County Historical Commission

ARCADIA
PUBLISHING

ISBN 978-1-4671-2712-7

Published by Arcadia Publishing
Charleston, South Carolina

Printed in the United States of America

Library of Congress Control Number: 2017936111

For all general information contact Arcadia Publishing at:
Telephone 843-853-2070
Fax 843-853-0044
E-mail sales@arcadiapublishing.com
For customer service and orders:
Toll-Free 1-888-313-2665

Visit us on the Internet at www.arcadiapublishing.com

To the Walker County residents who contributed to this project.

Contents

ACKNOWLEDGMENTS

The members of the Walker County Historical Commission began this project more than a decade ago. James Patton, Donna Coffen, Tom Rogers, and the other members of the commission's publication committee have been instrumental in getting this book completed. In addition, Carolyn Carroll, Brook Franks, Jami Horne, and Briana Weaver at Sam Houston State University have helped in various stages of the production process. Thanks to all those involved. All images in this collection appear courtesy of the Walker County Historical Commission.

Introduction

This project originated in 2004, when the City of Huntsville's Arts Commission awarded a grant to the Walker County Historical Commission for the accumulation, preservation, and publication of historic postcards from the county. James Patton, Donna Coffen, and Tom Rogers purchased postcards at various book and paper shows, antique shops, and historical events. Local citizens also donated dozens of cards to the historical commission to aid in this project. In 2016, the historical commission loaned the cards to the Thomason Special Collections Room at the Newton Gresham Library on the campus of Sam Houston State University. The cards were scanned by a university archivist and thereby permanently preserved in digital format. In addition, the 2004 grant called for the publication and public presentation of these historic postcards for the residents of Walker County and interested citizens across the area. It is hoped that the publication of this book will encourage the recovery of heretofore-unknown cards.

The postcards presented here are of critical significance to the history of Walker County. These postcards bring to light vital aspects of regional life in the first half of the 20th century. They provide some of the most significant documentation of the buildings, street scenes, and events in Walker County over the last 100 years, and in some cases are the only pictorial items that are left for us. Indeed, many of the places depicted on these postcards are now gone or greatly altered. Thus, these cards capture for us an important part of our collective past that is available in no other medium.

Chapter one of this book examines the critical role that Gen. Sam Houston and his wife, Margaret, played in the early history of Walker County. Sam Houston served as the victorious leader of Texian forces at the Battle of San Jacinto, first president of the Republic of Texas, and later governor and senator from Texas. Today, the Sam Houston Memorial Museum sits on 18 of the original 174 acres that Houston owned in Huntsville between 1847 and 1858. The museum grounds feature the Woodland Home, Steamboat House, and replicas of the Houstons' kitchen and law office. Additionally, historic log buildings have been relocated on the site in recent years.

Chapter two highlights the public buildings and private businesses that have shaped Walker County since the late 19th century. Postcards of the Walker County Courthouse, New Waverly's downtown district, the Dodge Train Depot, and the historic Huntsville Post Office of 1931 are key entries.

In the third chapter, postcards of local homes and churches are featured. Sallie Gibbs's large and grandiose Victorian home, built in 1895, was for years a Huntsville landmark. Likewise, the Josey-King home, the Wynne home, and the Gillaspie place served as prominent dwellings in the community. The occupants of these homes attended the county's earliest churches, including

First Methodist, First Baptist, First Presbyterian, and First Christian in Huntsville. There are also postcards from St. Joseph Catholic Church and St. Stephen Episcopal, as well as one of the Huntsville Church of Jesus Christ of Latter-day Saints.

Chapter four examines Sam Houston State University as it developed over the last century. Prominent buildings on the campus are featured. Old Main, constructed in 1889, serves as the most historic and revered early building. It was destroyed by fire in 1982, leaving the Austin College building and the Peabody Library as the oldest structures on campus. Additional postcards feature buildings on the quadrangle, including the early science building, which is now the Bobby K. Marks Administration Building.

In chapter five, postcards illustrating the development of the Texas State Penitentiary and criminal justice system are presented. A wide selection of images of the Walls Unit throughout the years is accompanied by pictorial cards showing outlying farms like the Wynne and Ellis Units. Another group of postcards showcases the prison rodeo, which began in 1931 and ended in 1986. The rodeo featured inmate cowboys and "free-world" entertainment, like John Wayne, Johnny Cash, and Dolly Parton.

Chapter six highlights the scenic outdoor opportunities available in Walker County. Huntsville State Park, the historic Lost Indian Camp, and Lake Raven are featured. In addition, there are postcards highlighting the all-female band the Goree Girls, as well as the Texas Prison Rodeo and the Texas Prison Museum. Other recent topics of interest include the construction of David Adickes's 77-foot Sam Houston statue on Interstate 45 and the dedication of the Ruth and Roy Blatchley Bell Tower at Sam Houston State University.

One

The Home of Gen. Sam Houston

Gen. Sam Houston, the first president of the Republic of Texas and later governor of the state, lived for many years in Huntsville. This postcard features Houston's home after it was sold to the Smead family and enlarged to serve as a boardinghouse for women at Sam Houston Normal College.

General Houston is seen here as he appeared around 1856, while serving as a US senator.

Sam and Margaret Houston's house, called Woodland Home, is seen here from the north side around 1910.

This beautiful postcard features the Houstons' home site around 1930. From left to right are the outdoor kitchen, home, and law office.

Martinus H. Stougaard is pictured in front of Woodland Home after it was restored in 1929. Note the stone fence and the plain style of the home.

The Houstons' Woodland Home, law office, and kitchen are pictured around 1935.

On this postcard, Woodland Home is pictured from the north after its 1929 restoration. Note the catalpa tree and coloring around the windows.

This colorful card shows Woodland Home from the north with a stone wall and catalpa tree.

Woodland Home is pictured from the north around the 1940s.

Woodland Home and Sam Houston's law office are pictured from the east prior to 1957.

Woodland Home is pictured during a rare snow in Huntsville around 1960.

Woodland Home is pictured in the spring during the early 1960s. This photograph showcases the restoration of the Greek Revival portico that had been on the house prior to the 1929 restoration. J.L. Clark suggested to museum director Grace Longino that the portico be restored after she discovered a c. 1899 photograph of the Smead boardinghouse. The portico was added in time for a 1957 story on Sam Houston that appeared in *McCall's* magazine.

The photograph for this postcard was taken by C.C. Springfield of Huntsville and showcases Woodland Home from the southwest corner.

Gough Photo Service of Houston, Texas, published this card of Huntsville's famous Woodland Home.

This Gough postcard from the 1960s features the white picket fence that was added to Woodland Home in the late 1930s. The original pickets for this fence were hand-cut and painted by students from Sam Houston Teachers College.

Sam Houston's Greek Revival home was photographed by Gough Photo Service around 1970.

Woodland Home is shown as it appears today after controversial changes were made in 1981.

Sam Houston's law office is seen from the south side around 1935. The photograph was taken by local photographer Joe Baker.

This photograph of the Woodland Home site shows Lake Oolooteka. The lake was named after Houston's friend John Jolly, the principal chief of the Cherokee Nation–West.

Sam Houston's Steamboat House
Huntsville, Texas

This model of the Steamboat House was created for the 1936 Texas Centennial and was originally displayed at the Julia Ideson Library in downtown Houston. The model shows the Steamboat House as it would have appeared in Houston's day, with an attached kitchen and outbuilding. Today, the model can be seen at the San Jacinto Monument in Houston.

Gen. Sam Houston died in the front downstairs bedroom of the Steamboat House in 1863. This postcard shows the house shortly after it opened to the public on the grounds of the Sam Houston Memorial Museum on March 2, 1937.

Dr. Rufus Bailey built the Steamboat House, which was intended as a wedding gift for his son Frank B. Bailey and his bride. The couple disliked the house, so it was available for Sam and Margaret Houston to rent when they returned from Cedar Point in 1861.

This postcard shows the Steamboat House as it appeared in the 1970s.

The Steamboat House was moved to the Sam Houston Memorial Museum grounds in 1936 and remains a key part of the site today.

This postcard from 1905 shows Gen. Sam Houston as "the Hero of San Jacinto" and "the Liberator of Texas."

The original gravesite of Sam Houston highlights the picket fence that his former slave, Joshua Houston, built following the general's death.

An early artistic representation shows Pompeo Coppini's monument to Sam Houston, which is located over his grave at Oakwood Cemetery in Huntsville. The monument was dedicated by Democratic statesman William Jennings Bryan on April 21, 1911, the 75th anniversary of the Battle of San Jacinto. The last two surviving veterans of San Jacinto attended the event, as did four of Houston's children.

The Houston Monument features Lady Victory to the left with an upside-down sword, Lady History to the right holding Henderson Yoakum's first volume of Texas history, and Sam Houston riding in battle. The upside-down torches mean the battle is over and victory is won. The laurel wreaths represent peace.

The Houston Monument arrived in Huntsville as 17 separate pieces of gray Texas granite. The Alamo Iron Works made the fence. The upside down Roman axes on the fence mean the battle is over. The plaster cast model for this fence is in the Alamo gift shop in San Antonio, Texas.

The Sam Houston Memorial Museum sits on 18 acres that Houston owned in Huntsville between 1847 and 1858. Students at Sam Houston Normal Institute initiated the movement to preserve the homestead in 1905. They moved Houston's Woodland Home and law office back to their original site in 1911, and the Texas legislature appropriated $15,000 for development of the site in 1927. The formal dedication of the museum was on May 3, 1929.

In 1936, the Texas Centennial Commission appropriated $35,000 for construction of the museum rotunda, which was designed to preserve and exhibit artifacts of the Houston era. The museum is owned and managed by Sam Houston State University.

The Sam Houston Memorial Museum has long played a role in educating schoolchildren about the Hero of San Jacinto.

Between 1936 and 1965, three wings were added to the Sam Houston Memorial Museum rotunda to house its permanent collections and exhibits.

This colorful Roslin & Company postcard depicts Tom Blue, General Houston's bodyguard in the Texas-Mexican War.

The Sam Houston Memorial Museum and complex were listed in the National Register of Historic Places, and Woodland Home was declared a national historic landmark in 1974.

The Sam Houston Memorial Museum includes 10 buildings, a natural woodland area, and several landscaped spaces. Lake Oolooteka is an artificial pond named in honor of Houston's adoptive Cherokee Indian father, John Jolly.

This photographic postcard shows Sam Houston Normal College as viewed from Lake Oolooteka on the grounds of the Sam Houston Memorial Museum.

Two

The County Courthouse and Street Scenes

This postcard features the fourth Walker County Courthouse, which was constructed in 1888. Architect Eugene T. Heiner designed the building and the iron fence (inside the wood fence), which was relocated to Oakwood Cemetery in 1912.

Construction of this courthouse, which was the fourth built in the county, became necessary when the main structure of the third courthouse burned down in 1888. All that remained was the grand jury house, which had been separate from the main structure and was used while preparations for a fourth courthouse were made.

In 1888, the Walker County Commissioners Court chose a Houston architect, Eugene T. Heiner, to design the fourth courthouse. A construction contract was given to N. Darling of Palestine, Texas. Building began in the late spring of 1888 and was completed that same year. The structure contained Victorian, Gothic, Renaissance, and Italianate elements, which had all been in Heiner's original design of the building.

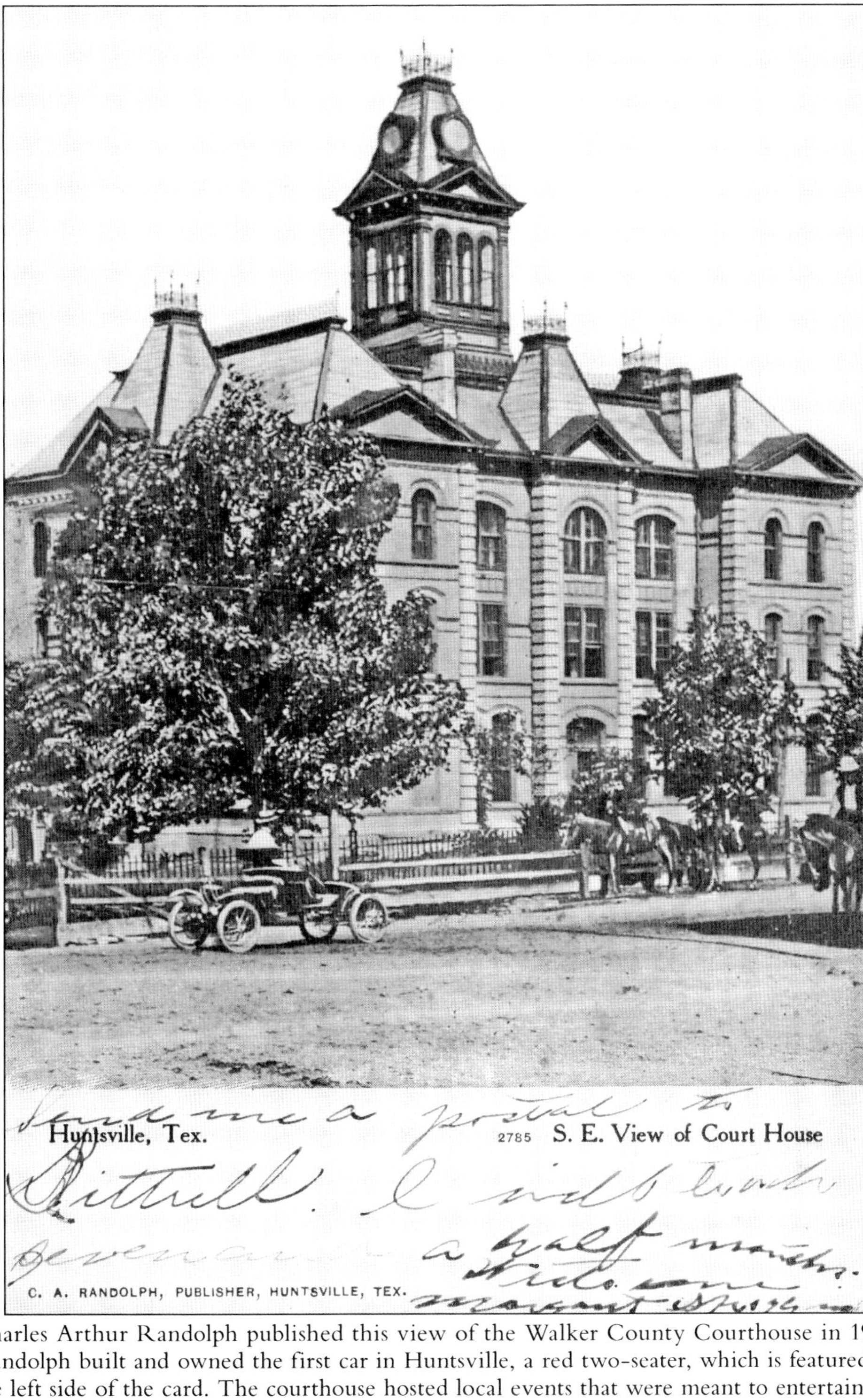

Charles Arthur Randolph published this view of the Walker County Courthouse in 1907. Randolph built and owned the first car in Huntsville, a red two-seater, which is featured on the left side of the card. The courthouse hosted local events that were meant to entertain the public, including the Walker County Fair of 1912 and a series of lectures that were sponsored by Texas A&M University in 1914.

This west-side view of the Walker County Courthouse shows the building in the 1930s. A storm damaged the former clock tower in the 1920s, and it was torn down. By 1968, this building was one of the 25 oldest courthouses in the state of Texas.

On December 24, 1968, fire once again struck the Walker County Courthouse. The roof, courtroom, and offices on the third floor were damaged. In a controversial move, the entire building was demolished and the current courthouse was constructed. Nevertheless, interested citizens may find an identical twin to this historic building in Wharton County.

This postcard shows an early image of the fifth and current courthouse of Walker County. The building was completed in September 1970 and is made of brick and steel, modern materials that were indicative of a new age. It remains at the center of downtown Huntsville on Courthouse Square.

This artistic depiction of the east side of Huntsville's square at the beginning of the 20th century highlights some of the local businesses then in operation. Stores run by H.F. Adickes and T.P. Robinson and a bakery, possibly owned by the Foster family, are prominent features.

This 1910 postcard offers one of the few remaining images of historic New Waverly. It features the local train depot and an arriving locomotive. The tracks to New Waverly were laid in 1872. Material goods, lumber, and agricultural products, as well as passengers, filled the train cars. Trains still travel through the town today, but passenger service has long been discontinued.

This postcard offers an early view of downtown New Waverly that showcases the town's mercantile operations and bank. By 1884, the town had a population of 150 residents and had several general stores, steam sawmills, a gristmill, two cotton gins, and two saloons.

VIEW OF EAST SIDE OF SQUARE, HUNTSVILLE, TEXAS.

WEST SIDE OF SQUARE, HUNTSVILLE, TEXAS.

This historic postcard features two views of Huntsville's downtown square around 1910. The card appeared with a collection of Huntsville scenes that could be purchased together. This card's top image shows the east side of the square looking north. In the distance, the 1907 Huntsville Public School building can be seen. The lower image shows the west side of the square looking north. Gibbs Brothers can be seen at lower right.

Edward King Goree, for whom the Goree Prison Farm is named, is pictured here around 1910. A Civil War veteran from Hood's Brigade, Edward King Goree was the brother of Thomas Jewett Goree. Mamie Rather Powell wrote a poem about Edward King Goree and the normal school girls who lived at the Howell Mayes Boarding House, which included the line, "This old man went to the boarding house and took the girls a riding in his buggie."

This 1909 postcard shows Normal Hill in Huntsville from the penitentiary. An International & Great Northern train is leaving town, and local landmarks can be seen behind its smoke. Old Main towers above the town at the top of the hill, with J.R. Irvine's two-story home below it.

This postcard shows a drugstore in New Waverly around 1910. A few years later, in 1914, New Waverly had a population of 500, as well as a bank, hotel, and a newspaper.

Issued in 1908, this C.A. Randolph postcard showcases many of the oldest buildings on the north side of Huntsville's square. The most notable structure, on the far left, was Gibbs National Bank, constructed in 1890. It became First National Bank in 1922 and remained in the same location until 1962.

The postmark on this postcard with a bird's-eye view of Huntsville is from 1914. The image is oriented to the south and shows the interior courtyard of the penitentiary, houses on Normal Hill, and Old Main at far right.

This linen postcard from the mid-1940s shows the grounds of Sam Houston's private farm. The card reads: "Here, on these grounds and in these houses, lived the Hero of Texas Independence, General Sam Houston. Here the old General sat and smoked the Peace Pipe with his Indian Friends who came to Huntsville to trade, here he sat as he watched his children grow to manhood."

The Corner Drug Store in Huntsville produced this black-and-white postcard in 1907.

This C.C. Springfield postcard showcases the Old Main Building and Museum at Sam Houston State Teachers College. The Santa Anna saddle today resides at Sam Houston Memorial Museum.

This photographic postcard features New Waverly State Bank, which was built in 1909 and capitalized at $40,000. The bank's motto was "Not as Large as the Largest, But as Strong as the Strongest." The bank was later renamed Citizens Bank of Texas and moved to Highway 75 and FM 1375 in New Waverly.

Sam Houston Memorial Drive was paved in 1936 for the Texas Centennial and repaved in 1986 for the Texas Sesquicentennial. The road leads from Eleventh Street to Sam Houston's grave on Ninth Street in Huntsville. At one time, it was the shortest highway in Texas.

This post office in Huntsville was completed in 1931, and federal offices operated in its basement. Built in the Mediterranean Revival style, it served until 1975. It now houses the Walker County district attorney's office.

The Houston & Great Northern Railroad established the town of Riverside in 1872. Cotton and timber were important commodities for the town, but the train remained crucial as well. This postcard shows a Trinity River bridge that was damaged by flooding in 1925.

Joe and Mable Baker built this beautiful motel in the early 1950s. It remains in its original location along Sam Houston Avenue. It may have been the first motel in Huntsville.

The Baker Motel has been renovated several times over the years. This postcard shows the property and its tree-lined parking lot during the 1960s.

This C.C. Springfield aerial view of Huntsville features the county courthouse, local businesses, and downtown homes. Likely taken on Rodeo Sunday, this photograph dates to the early 1950s.

A Holiday Inn opened in Huntsville in 1969. This artistic rendition falsely portrays what was actually built, but the hotel did serve thousands of visitors every year.

Dr. Joshua Allen Thomason gave this home to his daughter and her new husband, Rev. Jeremiah Ward, as a wedding present in 1872. Over a century later, the Junction Restaurant opened here in 1976. Today, the building serves as home to the 1836 Steakhouse.

This photographic postcard provides a view of Huntsville from the public school around 1910. The prominent building on the right is the fourth county courthouse; it still had a clock tower

at the time. The tallest building on the left is the entrance to the Texas Penitentiary.

This 1907 fishbowl view of Huntsville was produced for the Corner Drug Store. Oriented to the northwest, the photograph features First Baptist Church on the right and the county courthouse at center.

This March 1956 postcard features the Dodge Train Depot, W.O. Hopper's Lone Star Feed and Fertilizer, and the Humble gas station in the background. The Houston & Great Northern Railroad built the Dodge station in 1872. Dodge served as a junction for the Trinity Valley Southern Railway and International–Great Northern Railroad for 35 years beginning in 1901.

The Square Barbershop in Huntsville operated during the mid-20th century. Founded by Grady O. Bannon and Marvin Ballew, the barbershop boasted modern and up-to-date service. Later, Andy Anderson and Travis Corley operated the shop until 1975. Currently, this space serves as the dining room of Café Texan.

This, the original postcard produced for the Square Barbershop, is reversed. It was never distributed but is now held by the Walker County Historical Commission.

Abe Dabaghi and his partners founded the Café Raven in 1930. Located at the southeast corner of Sam Houston Avenue and Twelfth Street, the café boasted one of the first air-conditioned dining rooms between Dallas and Houston. It was named in honor of Sam Houston, who was popularly known as "the Raven." A French chef prepared food for locals and traveling dignitaries. The restaurant closed in 1969.

This postcard features Cox Funeral Home, a historic African American business at 1305 Thirteenth Street in Huntsville.

Three

Historic Homes, Churches, and Schools

Pine Crest, the home of Walter and Mary Gillaspie, was constructed in 1885. Located where Mance Park Middle School's gym sits today, the Gillaspie home was furnished with items made at the state penitentiary. Gillaspie's father, Capt. James Gillaspie, was the superintendent of the state prison system. This home burned down in November 1925, but various items from it survived.

This postcard, published by Huntsville's Corner Store, shows the home of Sallie Gibbs. Built by Will Hanby Randolph in 1895, the home featured stained-glass windows, marble accents, and iron fencing. Beautifully decorated, it served as the most ornate private home in Huntsville for many decades.

The 1895 Sallie Gibbs home was on the southeast corner of Eleventh Street and Avenue M in Huntsville. Sandford and Sallie Gibbs had previously owned a Greek Revival home in the same location; it was moved across the street to the current site of First National Bank.

After Sallie Gibbs's death in 1918, her oldest son, W.S. Gibbs Sr., and his wife, Annie, inherited the family home. The couple lived in the house until Annie's death in 1939. It then served as a boardinghouse and was demolished in 1951 as Champion Paper was preparing to lease it for offices.

This postcard, published by C.A. Randolph of Huntsville, shows the residence of J.R. Irvin. Designed by E.T. Earnest, the home sat on the northeast corner of Avenue J and Sixteenth Street. The home burned down around 1910. Col. A.T. McKinney later built a home on the same location, and Lone Star Hall on the campus of Sam Houston State University now occupies the site.

Sandford Gibbs gave this home to his niece Samuella Gibbs and her husband, Gustavus Adair Wynne, in 1883 as a wedding gift. This postcard shows the home around 1910, before renovations were made in 1912.

Originally built by Williamson Wynne, this home was remodeled and later occupied by county judge Patrick Henry Singeltary and his family. The home sat on Fifteenth Street between University Avenue and Avenue J in Huntsville.

This postcard features the Rev. Harry and Nannie May home in Huntsville. Reverend May was a Methodist circuit riding preacher. The home served as a boardinghouse on Avenue J between Sixteenth and Seventeenth Streets, where the William R. Powell Health Services and Counseling Center sits now. It burned down in 1918.

Pictured here is the home of Victor Hugo Pace and family. It sat on University Avenue and burned down in December 1983.

This postcard, published by the Corner Drug Store, features a home built around 1905 for H.Y. and Mary Robinson of Huntsville. It sat on the corner of Tenth Street and Sam Houston Avenue facing east. H.Y. Robinson owned a hardware store, and he and his wife were great supporters of the Methodist church. In fact, their sons gave property to the church.

The superintendent of the Texas prison system lived in this Italianate home near the Walls Unit. It was torn down in the early 1950s. Today, the Texas Department of Criminal Justice Conference Center occupies the site.

This beautiful home was built around 1895 by the Cotton States Building Company for Will and Kathleen Josey. Will's sister, Mollie Josey, later married J.R. King, and the couple bought the house. It was bricked in the 1920s and sits on the northeast corner of University Avenue and Fifteenth Street. Later, local entrepreneur George Russell purchased the Josey-King home and opened a museum there.

J.R. King operated a drugstore on the west side of the Huntsville square during the mid-20th century. He and his wife, Mollie Josey King, lived in this updated, bricked edition of the Josey-King home.

Loulie Estill designed the president's home at Sam Houston Normal Institute after the previous residence burned down around 1910. This home sat on the location of the current Alumni

Fountain near the west end of the Lowman Student Center on the campus of Sam Houston State University. The home was torn down in 1970.

William "Bill" Elkins is pictured on the front porch of his grandmother's home around 1910. The home sat on the southwest corner of Thirteenth Street and Avenue J. Later, it served as the Peters Hotel. In 1963, the property was deeded to Sam Houston State Teachers College, and was torn down in 1964.

James A. Thomason, a veteran of the War of 1812, settled in Huntsville in 1854. He built this home at 906 Avenue M in 1859. It has been in the Thomason-Eastham family for five generations. Today, it is a recorded Texas landmark known as the Whistler Bed and Breakfast.

This artistic rendition of the Wynne Home is available for purchase at the Wynn Home Arts Center's gift shop at 1428 Eleventh Street in Huntsville.

Local artist Betty Liles painted this beautiful interpretation of the Wynne Home Arts Center as it appears today. Her work was featured at the Wynne Home in 2011.

Published by C.A. Randolph, this photographic postcard features the Masonic temple in downtown Huntsville. Although the temple did not open until 1908, the Masons had long been active in Walker County. Leading members of the local community, including Sam Houston, Henderson Yoakum, and Alexander MacDonald, were Masons.

This photograph shows a crowd gathered for the funeral of Rev. Thomas Aloysius Bily (1859–1921) at St. Joseph's Catholic Church in New Waverly. The church had its origins in the post–Civil War era, when Polish immigrants migrated to the area to work in agricultural production. Rev. Felix Orzechowski established St. Joseph's in 1869, and it has served the local community for almost 150 years.

This postcard features the second building to serve as home to the First United Methodist Church in Huntsville. Established in 1842, the Methodist church is the oldest continuous congregation in Walker County.

The First Presbyterian Church in Huntsville was organized early in the city's history. The congregation constructed its first building in 1855 at the corner of Thirteenth Street and University Avenue. The initial structure was torn down in 1898 and replaced with the building pictured here.

The initial meetings of Huntsville's First Christian Church date to January 1854, when the congregation met in local houses. The church bought the former Cumberland Presbyterian Church in 1871. Later, this structure was removed, and in 1901, the congregation erected the building pictured here.

Early Baptists in Huntsville bought two plots of land for their first church in November 1852. Although the date of the initial building is unknown, First Baptist Church erected its sanctuary sometime in the mid-1850s. As the congregation grew, it needed additional space for services. In 1891, the church constructed its second building, which served the congregation until 1924, when it was torn down and replaced with the three-story brick building pictured here. In January 1954, a fire ripped through the building, destroying most of it. It now serves as Sunday school rooms and a chapel.

St. Stephen Episcopal Church traces its roots to the 1840s and 1850s. Laypeople initially led the church, but in 1871, Rev. Jeremiah Ward became rector. Two years later, the congregation consecrated its first church building. Although attendance remained small throughout the remainder of the 19th century, the church constructed a beautiful new building, pictured here, at Avenue L and Thirteenth Street in 1904.

In January 1913, the First United Methodist Church opened a new sanctuary and building in downtown Huntsville. Five years later, however, the church was gutted by fire. This postcard shows the renovated church, which opened in 1919 at the corner of Sam Houston Avenue and Eleventh Street.

The Church of Jesus Christ of Latter-day Saints began meeting in Huntsville as early as 1949. The congregation established its first church building in 1955, and membership increased dramatically during the 1970s. Since that time, the church has moved to Nineteenth Street and Avenue S, where it offers a kind welcome to visitors every week.

After the first public school in Huntsville burned down in 1906, the city constructed a beautiful two-story brick building that opened the following year. This school served white students in all grades and was at the corner of Eighth Street and Avenue K, on the site of the current Mance Park Middle School.

Despite the aesthetic beauty of the Huntsville Public School, officials ordered it torn down in 1963. It was replaced by newer schools that were built during the era of desegregation.

This building served as the public school in New Waverly, Texas, during the early part of the 20th century. James Patton, the former Walker County clerk and a member of the historical commission, remembers that his mother taught English and Spanish in this building.

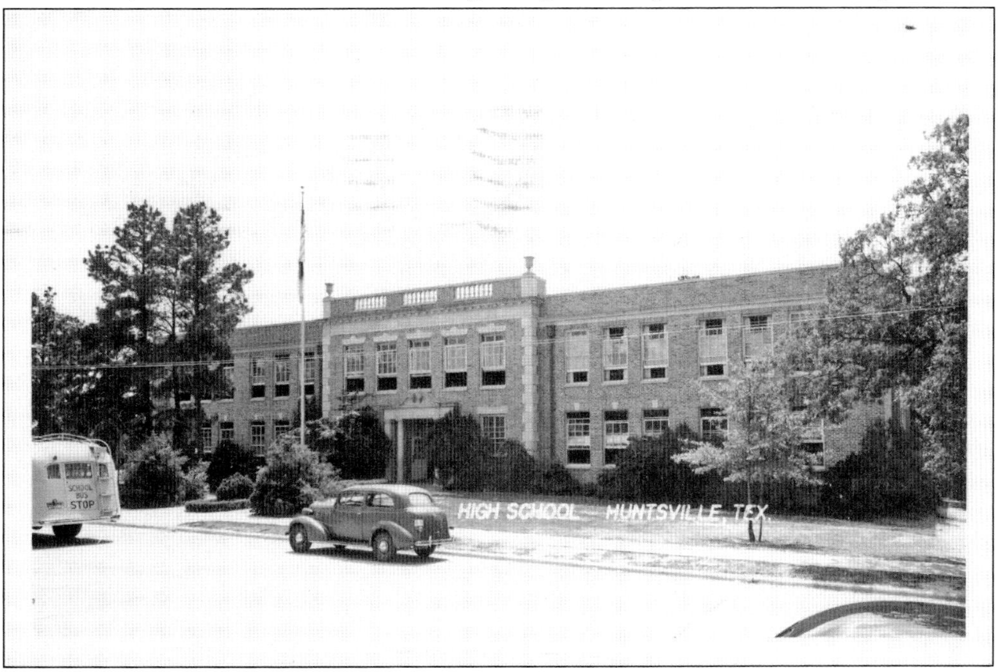

Huntsville High School was designed by Harry Payne and operated from 1931 to 1951. It then served as Huntsville Junior High until 1968. At that time, it was repurposed to function as an overflow wing of the high school during the desegregation process. All junior high students were sent to the former all-black Samuel Walker Houston High School on Highway 190. In 1979, the building pictured here closed; today, it serves as home to the Adickes Studio and Gallery.

Local artist Cynthia Reed painted this beautiful watercolor of the old Huntsville High School.

Four

Sam Houston State University

Established on April 21, 1879, Sam Houston Normal Institute prepared college students to teach in the public school system. The young people at Sam Houston loved the local campus, which featured a beautiful, two-story building called Old Main. Completed in 1890, Old Main had towering spires, stained-glass windows, and high-ceilinged rooms for events and classes.

Built on Capitol Hill behind Austin Hall, Old Main stood as the highest point in Huntsville and offered a beautiful view of the city's downtown. It also provided much-needed classroom and office space, as well as a new library and an auditorium that sat more than 1,200 people.

By 1923, Sam Houston Normal had 56 faculty members and nearly 1,100 students. Owing to the growth and development of the institution, the school changed its name to Sam Houston State Teachers College that year.

This view of Sam Houston Normal Institute features the Gothic-inspired Old Main building, Austin Hall behind Old Main, and Peabody Library on the left. The library, finished in 1902, was named in honor of George Peabody, a philanthropist who supported institutions of higher education around the country. This was the first Sam Houston building to be used exclusively as a library.

This postcard displays a rare view of Old Main from the back of Austin Hall. The buildings were built so close to one another that during construction of Old Main, the students were often distracted in their Austin Hall classrooms by the noise.

A young Sam Houston Normal Institute student bought this postcard from the local Corner Drug Store. On the back, he wrote to a friend in Jacksonville, Texas, that he was studying for a history exam that he had the next day.

This colorful print of Old Main highlights the English ivy that decorated the north side of the building. The ivy had to be removed in the 1950s due to the damage it caused to the building's mortar.

Sam Houston students often gathered near the north entrance to Old Main. In a common experience, they enjoyed interacting with Tripod the dog. Revered by all, Tripod lived on campus from 1948 to 1962 as the school's unofficial mascot.

In the early morning hours of February 12, 1982, Old Main was engulfed in flames. Despite the desperate attempts of fire fighters from as far away as Navasota and Onalaska, the flames could not be stopped. The building was destroyed, and in 1987, a memorial park was established in its place.

Today, Austin Hall is the university's showpiece, standing as the oldest building on campus. The cornerstone of the building was laid on June 24, 1851. It took two years to complete the building, but once done, it could be seen atop its hill from a great distance. Austin Hall served as

the principal structure for Austin College from 1853 to 1876. At that time, the college moved to Sherman, Texas; three years later, Austin Hall became part of Sam Houston Normal Institute.

This postcard, produced for the Corner Drug Store, features an 1881 image of students celebrating the completion of the third-floor addition to Austin Hall. The mansard roof shown here was in place from 1881 to 1927.

Published by Springfield News, this postcard calls Huntsville the "Athens of Texas" because of the town's "culture and refinement" and the "friendliness of its people." Displayed on the front of the card are prominent buildings on Sam Houston's campus, including Caroline Belvin Hall, Andrew Jackson Hall, and the administration building.

SAM HOUSTON STATE TEACHERS COLLEGE. SCIENCE HALL. HUNTSVILLE. TEXAS. 101175

In 1931, a female student sent this postcard displaying the Science Building to her friend Miss B. Hobson in Garner, Texas. The student wrote that school had been in session for a week, and that she was enjoying "every minute of it."

1016 CAMPUS, SAM HOUSTON STATE TEACHERS COLLEGE, HUNTSVILLE, TEXAS

This postcard shows the historic quadrangle on Sam Houston's campus. Students walking next to the administration building appear to be headed towards Austin Hall, which sits hidden behind the trees.

The caption on this postcard reads "Sam Houston State Normal Library, Huntsville, Texas," and the image highlights Old Main. Prior to the construction of the separate Peabody Library, the first floor of the Old Main building was used for the library.

Sold at the Huntsville Corner Drug Store, this postcard displays the Peabody Memorial Library after its completion in 1902. Designed in the shape of a cross, the library was complete with a spacious reading room, stained-glass windows, and even a fireplace. Unfortunately, after just 25 years of service, the library had become too small and was relegated to other uses, including housing the university archives for a short time. Renovations to the building were carried out in the 1990s, and since its rededication, it has functioned as a venue for receptions and special events.

The three-story Science Building was constructed in 1916 along the historic quadrangle at Sam Houston Normal Institute. It was the sixth permanent structure to appear on campus, and today it serves as the Bobby K. Marks Administration Building, which is home to the offices of the president, vice presidents, and the registrar.

Loretta Ansdell's mother sent this postcard home to her daughter on October 5, 1937, while traveling with her husband through Huntsville on their way to Galveston. She reflected on the local county fair and said that she was "having a nice time." The front of the postcard shows Belvin Hall, the first all-female student residence. It was named in honor of Caroline Belvin, a beloved former dean of women at the college.

Depicted in beautiful color on this postcard is the Manual Training Building, later the Industrial Arts Building, which opened in 1910. This two-story redbrick building was the fourth permanent structure on Sam Houston's campus. It served a variety of purposes over 70 years before being demolished in October 1982.

Published by the Huntsville and Walker County Chamber of Commerce in 1943, this postcard shows a side view of the biology and home economics building at Sam Houston State Teachers College.

This postcard from the 1960s looks northeast from Sam Houston Avenue toward the Farrington Building, which had an observatory on its roof (far right).

Published by the Springfield News Company of Huntsville, this postcard features three of the dormitories at Sam Houston State Teachers College. Jackson Hall, pictured on the left, sits to the west of the main campus and was opened in 1940. Elliott Hall, shown at the bottom, was the third student dorm at Sam Houston. And Belvin Hall, on the right, was an all-female residence hall.

This postcard offers an aerial view of Old Main and Sam Houston's historic quadrangle from the 1970s.

On this postcard, two female students stand in the portico of Elliott Hall wearing matching pink-and-black attire. An all-female dormitory, this four-story building offered bedrooms in varying color schemes, a dining room, and a large foyer. In 1974, the dorm was renovated, and it continues to house students today.

Published by the View Gram company of Amarillo, Texas, this postcard shows the South Gate to Sam Houston State Teachers College. The brick pillars were a graduation gift from the class of 1934, and the metal archway sign was a gift from the 1935 class.

Five

The Texas Prison System and Rodeo

Pictured here is the Texas State Penitentiary in Huntsville, which opened in 1849 and is commonly known as the Walls Unit. This Gothic Revival building was the second structure on the site and was designed by Eugene T. Heiner in 1895.

The clock pictured at the top of the Walls Unit was designed by Hawley and Morgan of Dallas. The two men married Huntsville women while working in the local community to complete the clock project.

The Texas electric chair, "Old Sparky," was installed at the Walls Unit in 1924. Over 40 years of use, the chair carried out 361 executions. It was replaced by lethal injection. Today, the chair is on display at the Texas Prison Museum in Huntsville.

This southeast view of the Texas Penitentiary depicts the prison labor system as it operated in the late 19th century. In 1853, the Texas government approved an appropriation of $35,000 to establish a cotton and woolen mill inside the Walls Unit to gain additional revenue and offset the prison's operational costs. According to Donald R. Walker, "prison officials believed they were accomplishing a dual objective: the work itself instilled habits of discipline, self-restraint, and responsibility, while the profits from the labor helped repay the prisoners' debt to society."

This uncommon postcard, published by J. Robert King of Huntsville, features the old wagon shop inside the Texas Penitentiary.

The Texas Penitentiary provided electricity to Sam Houston Normal Institute from 1891 to 1911. At that time, the city of Huntsville received electrical service, and the school went off the prison's grid.

This postcard features the Texas Penitentiary before 1942, when the building was remodeled with red wire brick.

This early-20th-century postcard showcases three homes that served the officials of the Texas State Penitentiary. It is believed that two of these homes still survive.

"Dear teacher this is the picture of our home," reads the inscription on the back of this postcard showing the residence of the penitentiary's financial agent. The home of the young letter writer was on the corner of Twelfth Street and Avenue I.

It is unclear who sent this 1907 postcard, but its message indicates that it was from a resident in the administration building. "This is our home. First floor is offices, others is ours. We are well pleased here. People are so lovely to us." There is no mention of the noise from the daily tolling of the bells for prison roll call, but that sound remains common today.

Ethel Oliphant of Waco, Texas, received this postcard from a cousin in 1907. The writer described the featured house as the "Pen[itentiary] House where Miss Mattie Baker lived." Mattie's father was Searcy Baker, a high-ranking official of the prison system.

This postcard features the flower gardens and fruit trees that grew inside the Walls Unit during the early part of the 20th century.

At one time, the Texas Penitentiary offered not only flower gardens and fruit trees but also its own full-service hospital.

In 1932, Miss Crow of Dallas received this postcard from one of her "dearest girlfriends," who signed her name mysteriously "3 guesses." It is unknown why she chose to send a postcard displaying the engine room at the state penitentiary, but she did not like the area. "Help, come get me, I don't like this place," she said.

This postcard, published by the Huntsville and Walker County Chamber of Commerce, highlights the remodeled administration building after 1942. The back preprinted message notes that this building was where all the convicts were formally checked in and processed.

Pvt. G.W. Aker sent this postcard to his parents in 1943 showing the arrival of the "Goodbye Wagon" at the penitentiary. As he described it, the wagon "looks like a rolling cell" and was "about 20 feet long" and made of "armor and bars."

This aerial view of the Texas Penitentiary features the old administration building, the prison rodeo complex, and prison official residences around 1939.

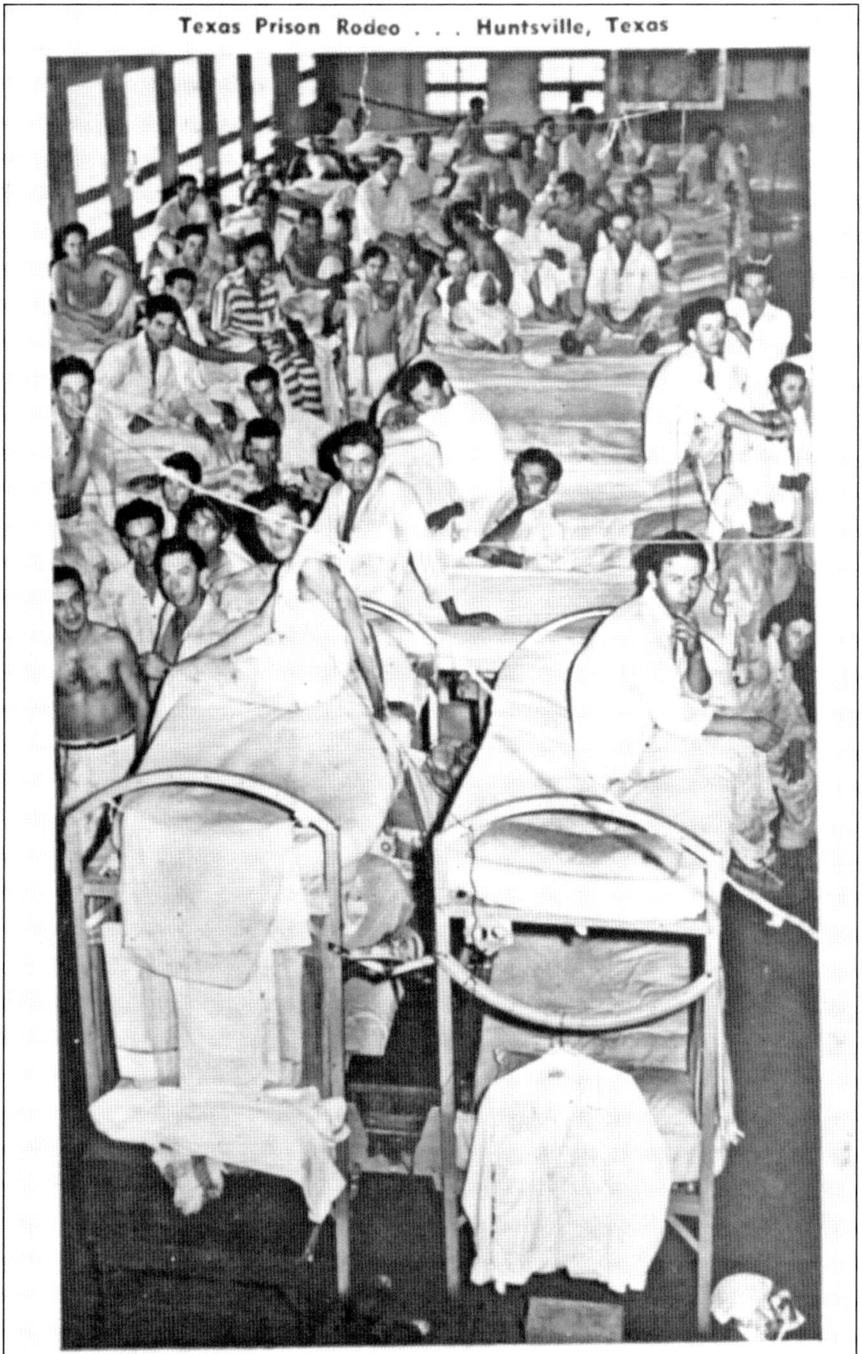

Inmates from the penitentiary stare into the camera on this postcard advertising the Texas Prison Rodeo. On the back, the preprinted message reads, " 'Sure we're ready to go,' say these inmates. Anything for a trip to the prison rodeo at Huntsville." Unfortunately, the sender, passing through town on July 9, 1950, was unable to enjoy the show, which occurred every Sunday in October.

Five sights in Huntsville are showcased on this postcard, produced by Springfield News in Huntsville. Clockwise from top left are the Goree Prison Farm for Women, a busy penitentiary with its first design, the 1931 post office, and the fourth Walker County Courthouse. At center is the Wynne Prison Farm, which in 1883 became the first prison farm established by the state.

This postcard shows the communications tower that Walker County residents would call to announce a fire or other calamity. Manned 24 hours a day, seven days a week, the tower office, called Number I Picket, appears just in front of the penitentiary. The operator of the tower office could then alert law enforcement through an emergency siren.

This J.D. Dickinson photographic postcard shows a southeast view of the Walls Unit in the 1970s.

This postcard, published by View Gram in Amarillo, displays a large grassy section in front of the Walls Unit and a hanging banner advertising the prison rodeo.

In 1961, a couple bought this postcard while traveling through Huntsville. They stopped at the prison craft shop, which provided inmate-made belts, wallets, purses, and toys for sale.

"A familiar sight to rodeo fans each October," reads the preprinted message on the back of this postcard. Launched in 1931, the rodeo showcased the talents of several hundred inmates, professional rodeo entertainers, and many celebrity acts over the years, including Johnny Cash, Dolly Parton, and Willie Nelson. The last rodeo was held on October 26, 1986.

The Ellis Unit, formerly part of the Smither Farm, is located 18 miles northeast of Huntsville. This maximum-security prison farm covers 11,672 acres and houses a population of more than 1,500 inmates. It is also the location of death row.

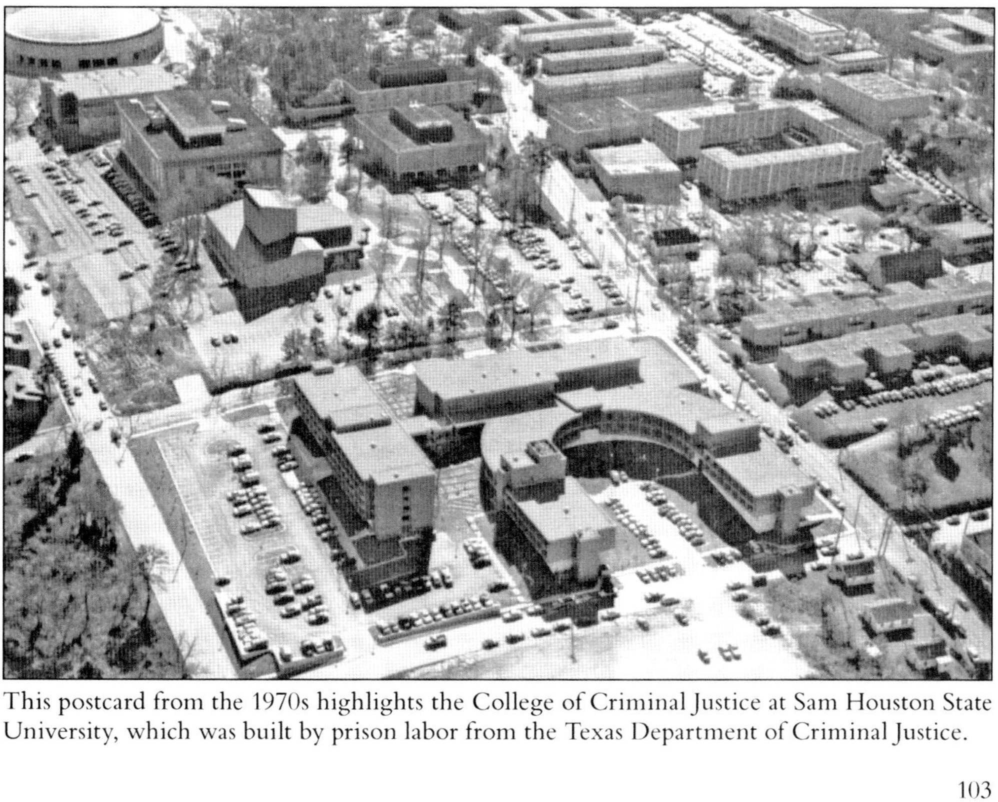

This postcard from the 1970s highlights the College of Criminal Justice at Sam Houston State University, which was built by prison labor from the Texas Department of Criminal Justice.

Published by Don R. Bartels in McAllen, Texas, this postcard was designed to advertise the Texas Prison Rodeo in its 27th year of operation. Crowd size grew annually, and in some years, attendance exceeded 100,000 people.

Inmate performers took great risks to participate in the Texas Prison Rodeo.

Seeing a horse buck off a rider was a common sight at the "Wildest Show Behind Bars." This postcard displays a prisoner attempting to hang on tight as his horse pulls his back feet high off the ground. It is easy to imagine the cheers and shouts from the crowd.

"One way—but not the approved way—to dismount from a bronc in the Texas Prison Rodeo," reads the back of this postcard, published by Springfield News. Beyond the standard rodeo events, the prison rodeo included "wild cow milking, calf belling, goat roping, wild mare milking, and bull dogging."

The chariot race, displayed on this postcard, was "a hilarious feature of each performance" at the Texas Prison Rodeo. In this image, two rodeo clowns are being pulled in their chariot, named "Strum Buggy."

Roman bareback riding, displayed on this postcard, was a feature of the rodeo. Another favorite event was the Hard Money competition, in which 40 inmates dressed in red shirts were placed in the arena with a bull. A sack of money was tied between the bull's horns. The inmate who was lucky enough to get the sack first won the money inside.

This postcard, published by Don R. Bartels in McAllen, Texas, advertised the crafts and souvenirs built by the inmates in the Texas Penitentiary. The preprinted message on the back read, "Gifts displayed and sold at the Inmate Handicraft Gift Shop are made by the inmates in their spare time and 85% of the receipts go into the inmates' trust fund. Leathercraft, gem-cutting, silvercraft, painting and woodworking are but a few of the crafts displayed."

This 1956 postcard displays a "convict cowboy" as an advertisement for the Texas Prison Rodeo, referred to as the "wildest, wooliest rodeo" around. This figure, as well as an advertisement and schedule for the local sporting events, was displayed in front of the Walker County Courthouse in the fall.

Six

Scenic Walker County

An African American unit of the Civilian Conservation Corps constructed Huntsville State Park in the late 1930s, during the Great Depression. The 2,083-acre park opened to the public in 1938.

Raven Lodge, a group recreation hall, was constructed by Unit 1823 of the Civilian Conservation Corps. It remains open for events today.

Fun activities at Huntsville State Park include canoeing, swimming, and fishing in Lake Raven, a 210-acre man-made lake. Over 50 native magnolia trees had to be cut down to create the lake.

Raven Lodge at Huntsville State Park has hosted many events over the years. Weddings, birthday parties, and family reunions often take place at the park.

Here is a rare peek inside Raven Lodge in the 1960s, when the building featured a concession stand and dining room for park guests.

Families often traveled to Huntsville State Park from Houston, Dallas, and other urban areas in East Texas. In fact, Huntsville State Park was, along with Garner Parker at Uvalde, one of the most visited sites in the state park system.

Children enjoy the playgrounds at swimming holes in Huntsville State Park. There are miles of hiking trails, beautiful spots for photographs, and picnic tables for meals by the lake.

Huntsville State Park, operated by Texas Parks and Wildlife, is located just south of Huntsville off Interstate 45 on Park Road 40.

Huntsville State Park remains a place to get away and unwind while enjoying scenery and wildlife.

This scenic bird's-eye view of Huntsville shows the iconic Old Main building at Sam Houston State Normal College around the beginning of the 20th century.

This aerial view of Huntsville was published H.G. Zimmerman and Company of Chicago.

The Texas pecan is one of Huntsville's most common in-town tree species. Planting the trees in town ensured that locals would enjoy a harvest of nuts.

This postcard introduced visitors to Lost Indian Camp, a recreational center for children that operated from 1955 to 1974. At the top of the card, covered wagons with campers sit on the bank of the Trinity River where the Old San Antonio and La Bahia Roads crossed the Trinity. On the bottom, campers feed Hiawatha, the camp mascot.

Lost Indian Camp featured a beautiful paddock swimming pool that was 80 by 40 feet. The children enjoyed swimming against a scenic background of giant oak trees laden with Spanish moss.

The main lodge at Lost Indian Camp sat atop a burial ground for the Bidai Indian tribe. Two Native American skeletons were unearthed here in the mid-1950s and inspected by Dr. T.N. Campbell, an anthropologist at the University of Texas, Austin.

This close-up shot of the lodge at Lost Indian Camp highlights the location where two Native American skeletons were found. The back of the postcard says that one of the skeletons was displayed in a rock tomb in the basement of the lodge.

Children at Lost Indian Camp enjoyed fishing for bass and perch in the local lake. Youngsters participated in other outdoor activities including hiking, archery, and exploring.

Local artist Cynthia Reed painted this view of Raven Lake at Huntsville State Park. It highlights the natural beauty of the area as well as the tranquility of the lake and park.

Lake Livingston is a popular recreational area for fishing, hunting, camping, and boating enthusiasts. It is fed by the Trinity River.

Gen. Sam Houston's grave marker is visited by many guests, especially on March 2, which commemorates both Houston's birthday and Texas Independence.

Like Sam Houston's grave marker, the Steamboat House remains a popular tourist attraction, especially during the spring, when flowers and trees are in bloom.

This 1908 postcard was published by C.A. Randolph of Huntsville. Although Old Main burned down in 1982, guests to town still visit the memorial ruins at the site.

The buildings pictured on this mid-century postcard no longer serve their original purpose. The one-time post office has now been converted into the Walker County district attorney's office, and the former high school now serves as an art studio for local artist David Adickes.

In 1969, Holiday Inn opened as the principal lodging facility for visitors to Walker County. It featured a beautiful swimming pool and large open courtyard. Today, the La Quinta hotel sits on the location.

Shortly after the turn of the 21st century, local artist Cynthia Reed painted this postcard of Fair on the Square, a cultural and arts event in Walker County.

Between acts at the Texas Prison Rodeo, the Goree Girls and supporting musicians entertained the large crowds who visited town in the 1950s.

The Texas Prison Museum opened in 1989 on the Huntsville square. The museum moved to a larger location at the intersection of US 75 and Interstate 45 in 2002. It offers an intriguing glimpse into the lives of the state's imprisoned citizens.

In 1986, Huntsville celebrated its sesquicentennial anniversary. This quilt, displayed at city hall, showcases Sam Houston's home site, local churches, and Sam Houston State University, among other sites of local interest.

The Ruth and Roy Blatchley Bell Tower was dedicated at Sam Houston State University on October 15, 2005.

Dan Phillips is a local architect and builder who leads Phoenix Commotion, a building initiative created to prove that constructing homes with recycled and salvaged material has a viable place in the building industry. Each one of his more than 20 homes is unique. His project targets single parents, artists, and families with low incomes. Pictured here is his recently opened Boot House on Eleventh Street in Huntsville.

This modern postcard compares the famous Sam Houston statute on I-45 with other well-known landmarks. The Sam Houston statute stands 77 feet tall and welcomes visitors from Houston to Huntsville.

This mold of Sam Houston's face sits in a small amphitheater near the base of the statue on I-45. It serves as a popular location for photographs by tourists to the area.

This 77-foot, illuminated statue of Sam Houston can be seen from six miles away. David Adickes completed the likeness of the Texas general in 1994, and it remains the tallest statue of an American hero in the world today.